Chinese Puzzles

Games for the Hands and Mind

Traditional Chinese puzzles
from the *Yi Zhi Tang* collection

Wei Zhang and Peter Rasmussen　張衛　雷彼得

Photography by Niana Liu　劉念

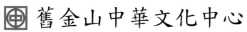 舊金山中華文化中心
CHINESE CULTURE CENTER OF SAN FRANCISCO

中國傳統益智遊戲

藝智堂收藏

Editorial Direction
Abby Chen
Program Director
Chinese Culture Center of San Francisco

Text
Wei Zhang and Peter Rasmussen
www.chinesepuzzles.org

Photography and Design
Niana Liu
www.nianaliu.com

Published on the occasion of the exhibition *Chinese Puzzles: Games for the Hands and Mind*, presented as part of the *Modern Classics Exhibition Series* at the Chinese Culture Center of San Francisco from July 22 through October 11, 2008.

The exhibition *Chinese Puzzles: Games for the Hands and Mind* was made possible by generous support from the Walter & Elise Haas Fund, the Vincent Woo Foundation, the San Francisco Foundation, Union Bank of California, and Grants for the Arts.

The Chinese Culture Center of San Francisco is a major community-based non-profit organization established in 1973 to foster the understanding and appreciation of Chinese and Chinese American art, history and culture in the United States.

ISBN 978-1-58886-101-6

Chinese Culture Center of San Francisco
750 Kearny Street, 3rd Floor
San Francisco, California 94108
www.c-c-c.org

Distributed worldwide by
Art Media Resources, Inc.
1507 South Michigan Avenue
Chicago, Illinois 60605
info@artmediaresources.com
www.artmediaresources.com

Contents 目録

Foreword

I met Wei Zhang and Peter Rasmussen in 1997, when they came to the Asian Art Museum of San Francisco with a box of ivory puzzles. There were fascinating objects in the box, including a small set of tangrams and two books of figures to create with them. There was also a nine linked rings puzzle. To untangle the nine rings from the loop is fiendishly difficult and involves 341 moves. A similar set of puzzles was illustrated in one of the books on the China Trade. I located the book and image, and I found out that the ivory puzzles were created in Canton during the 19th century and were made for the foreign market. Our friendship began from there, and from this first find the two collectors went on to amass a large collection of antique Chinese puzzles.

Puzzles have a long history in China and are designed to challenge the mind and improve the manual dexterity of young and old alike. Wei and Peter collected avidly and wisely. Not only do they collect puzzles, they also collect objects made in the shapes of puzzles. Tangrams fascinated them, and they found tables made in the shapes of tangrams, candy dishes in similar shapes, with examples in porcelain as well as in Yixing stoneware, lacquerware and wood.

Chinese Puzzles: Games for the Hands and Mind is more than just an exhibition of toys. Many of the puzzles are also art objects in the classical tradition and are of the highest workmanship. Wei and Peter enjoy serious research on their collection, and in their quest for knowledge they found Chinese documents, illustrations and first-hand accounts that helped them to place the objects in their historical contexts.

This is not the usual exhibition where people come to simply enjoy the art works. There are tables where one can stop and play with modern versions of the puzzles. The puzzles may look deceptively easy to untangle, but painful experience taught me that they are not. I remember well when two curators of the Asian Art Museum were given a simple wire puzzle in Shanghai by the granddaughter of the famous puzzle maker Ruan Liuqi. During the three-hour train ride from Shanghai to Nanjing, the curators took turns trying to untangle the two wires, and they were totally frustrated. The puzzle remained unsolved until it arrived in San Francisco, where the daughter of one of the curators untangled it in less than a minute.

Chinese Puzzles is a unique and exciting exhibition, and it will surely bring much enjoyment to viewers of all ages.

Terese Tse Bartholomew
Curator Emeritus of Himalayan Art and Chinese Decorative Art
Asian Art Museum of San Francisco

前言

我在一九九七年認識張衛和雷彼得夫婦。當時，他們帶來一套象牙益智遊戲來舊金山亞洲藝術館給我看。這套益智遊戲非常有趣，有七巧板和一套用七巧板作圖的書；還有九連環，要解開這個九連環可不容易，需要解 341 步！ 類似的益智游戲在一本早期中西貿易的書中也有介紹。書中提到這些象牙玩具是十九世紀廣州製作，並外銷到西方。我們之間的友誼由此開始。他們的古董益智游戲收藏也是從這一套象牙益智游戲開始，發展到現在可觀的數量。

益智遊戲在中國歷史悠久。它們不僅用於益智，還有助於動手，老少咸宜。張衛和雷彼得熱中而明智地收藏古董益智遊戲。除了古董益智遊戲外，他們還收藏有益智遊戲圖形的器具和物品。因為喜歡七巧遊戲，除七巧板外，他們還收藏了七巧桌，瓷器和宜興紫砂的七巧盤及漆器和木制的七巧盤。

這個展覽中的益智遊戲不僅僅是玩具，很多還是中國傳統工藝的精品。張衛和雷彼得愛好研究他們的藏品。他們找到很多文獻，圖案，和第一手的資料，瞭解這些益智遊戲的歷史背景。

和其它展覽不同的是，觀眾們在這裡不僅僅觀賞精美的古典益智遊戲，他們還可以在互動台上親自動手，玩賞新製益智遊戲。有些益智遊戲看上去十分簡單，但是，我自身的經驗告訴我並非如此。記得有一次在上海，著名巧環老藝人阮劉琪的孫女給了我一個巧環遊戲。在從上海到南京的三個多小時的火車上我和另一個亞洲藝術博物館的同事怎樣努力也解不開這個巧環。最後，回到舊金山，這個巧環還是沒開解。可是，當這個巧環到了我的女兒手裡，不到一分鐘就給解開了！

這是一個與眾不同的展覽，是一個讓人們賞心悅目的展覽。

謝瑞華
舊金山亞洲藝術博物館 中國裝飾工藝及西藏部 主任（退休）

Introduction

Welcome to the fascinating world of Chinese puzzles!

In China, traditional puzzles are called intelligence games *(yizhi youxi)* and are valued as tools for training the mind in creative and logical thinking.

The tangram puzzle, in which seven geometrical shapes are arranged to form figures, is called "the seven ingenious pieces" *(qiqiao ban)* in Chinese. Tangrams were invented over 200 years ago and became immensely popular among Chinese of all ages and social status. Soon a tangram craze swept across the world — much as Rubik's Cube did in our own era.

During the second half of the 19th century, a scholar-official named Tong Xiegeng invented a 15-piece variation of tangram that he used to illustrate verses of classical poetry. This puzzle, which Tong called "enhancing intelligence pieces" *(yizhi ban)*, was especially popular among scholars, and Tong went on to publish eight volumes containing his 15-piece constructions of 1000 Chinese characters.

The nine linked rings *(jiulianhuan)* is another traditional puzzle known throughout China and the world. The solution to this puzzle — in which nine rings must be removed from a looped handle — requires 341 moves. The moves follow a sequence that soon becomes embedded in the solver's mind. The mathematics underlying the solution is frequently used to illustrate recursion in mathematics and computer science.

The Chinese version of the sliding block puzzle is named Huarong Pass *(Huarong Dao)* and is based on the story of a battle that occurred just prior to the Three Kingdoms period. Burr puzzles, which are constructed out of interlocking rods, are called Lu Ban locks *(Lu Ban suo)* after the patron saint of carpentry. Chinese puzzle rings and bracelets made of several linked bands probably arrived in China over the Silk Road from Western Asia. They are easily taken apart but difficult to reassemble.

In addition to traditional puzzles, there are locks and boxes that were created to secure valuables — and which can be very challenging to open. Traditional Chinese locks can have hidden keyholes or require many steps to open; wooden boxes can have hidden locking mechanisms; and cabinets and desks can contain secret compartments.

Puzzle vessels function in ways that are counter-intuitive. Bottom-filling pots *(dao liu hu)* are filled through a hole in the bottom, but when they are turned upright nothing spills out. Fairness cups *(gong dao bei)* will hold liquid to a certain level, but if filled past that level every drop flows out through a hole in the cup's bottom. How do these vessels work?

And, finally, visual puzzles don't require one to take apart or put together anything — they're simply for contemplation. The Buddhist grottos of Dunhuang contain images of three rabbits, each of which has two ears but have a total of only three ears among them *(see www.threerabbits.net)*. A related image consists of four boys sharing two heads and two sets of appendages. How can this be? And what do these images mean?

We now invite you to view the *Yi Zhi Tang* collection of Chinese puzzles through the eyes and lens of Niana Liu, a young painter/photographer/designer from China who now makes her home in San Francisco. We have been privileged to work with Niana as she made her own discoveries in the world of Chinese puzzles and as she shared her unique perspective with us.

Wei Zhang and Peter Rasmussen
Berkeley, California

簡介

歡迎您來訪引人入勝的中國益智遊戲世界！

在中國，益智遊戲不僅用於娛樂，還用來提高人們的智力和邏輯思維能力。

益智遊戲七巧板由七塊幾何板組成，用來拼成各種圖形。七巧遊戲出現在兩百多年前，在中國十分流行。當它傳到國外後，和近代的 Rubik 立方體一樣，很快就風靡世界。

在十九世紀中葉，一位叫童叶庚的學者在七巧的基礎上發明了十五巧，並用其為古典詩句配圖作畫。童叶庚將他的發明稱作"益智板"。益智板在文人中很快流行開來。童叶庚後來又用他的十五塊益智板拼出千字文出版。

九連環是另一個著名中國益智遊戲。要將所有九個連環從環柄上解出需要解 341 步。解環的步驟是很有規律的，一旦理解學會，就能按規律解環。九連環中的數學原理也很重要，在一些數學和計算機的書中會用九連環作例題。

華容道是中國式的滑塊遊戲。這個遊戲以三國時期的一場著名的戰爭命名。遊戲中的滑塊用三國時期的人物作代表。這個遊戲有時也稱作"捉放曹"。

魯班鎖是一組中間凹凸的木塊，它們可以拼成一個立體的結構。這個遊戲被稱之為魯班鎖，是因為魯班是中國建築業和木工的祖師爺。

中國的連環戒指和手鐲由相連的銀質環體組成。它們很可能由絲綢之路從西亞流傳到中原。連環戒指或手鐲一旦散開後，將其還原卻十分不易。

傳統機關鎖具也內涵益智。它們有的鎖孔隱蔽，有的沒有鑰匙，有的雖然有鎖孔和鑰匙，但是要將鑰匙插入鎖孔卻很不容易。要開啟這些機關鎖需要很多步驟。

益智容器初看會讓人們不可思議。倒流壺要從壺的底部註酒，放正後，酒卻不會流出。公道杯內的酒水要適量，如果註入太多，所有的酒水就會全部從杯底的小孔流出。它們的原理是什麼呢？

最後，我們看看益智圖案。在中國敦煌窟穴裡的壁畫上有一些三兔圖形，每隻兔子有兩隻耳朵，但是，三隻兔子一起卻共有三隻耳朵(參看http://www.threerabbits.net)。和這個圖形類似的還有四喜圖，在四喜圖中的四個孩子由兩個頭和兩雙肢體組成。這個圖形是怎樣的呢？

我們誠摯地邀請您通過攝影師劉念的眼睛和鏡頭觀賞藝智堂中國傳統益智遊戲的收藏。劉念是來自中國的年輕藝術家，現住舊金山。她擅長繪畫，攝影及藝術設計。我們有幸和劉念合作，並通過她獨特的眼光欣賞中國傳統益智遊戲之美。

藝智堂　張衛 雷彼得
美國加利福尼亞州伯克利

1. Tangram

Tangram is China's most famous puzzle. Its Chinese name is *qiqiao ban*, which means "seven ingenious pieces." The seven flat pieces consist of two large triangles, one medium triangle, two small triangles, one square and one parallelogram — and all seven tangram pieces can be arranged to form a square. Along with the tangram pieces is a collection of outline diagrams in the shapes of animals, human figures, landscapes and objects. The objective of the puzzle is to place all seven pieces on a flat surface to form the same shape as one of the diagrams. Tangram originated in the late 18th to early 19th century and may have been based on sets of tables made in geometrical shapes. The earliest known tangram book was published by Sang Xia Ke in 1813.

七巧板是中國最著名的益智遊戲。七巧由七個幾何形板組成。分別是：兩個大三角、一個中三角、兩個小三角、一個正方形和一個平行四邊形。通常，這七塊板在一起拼成一個正方形。七巧遊戲包括一副七巧板和一些七巧圖形：有器物、山水、動物和不同姿態的人物。人們需要用所有七塊板根據圖題要求拼組成各種圖形，七巧創於十八世紀末、十九世紀初，可能是由幾何形拼桌演變而來。現有最早的七巧書是桑下客在 1813 年所著。

天然巧合 《吳有如畫寶》
Perfect fit, ca. 1890
Wu Youru (Chinese, d. 1893)
From *Complete prints of Wu Youru*, Shanghai, 1909

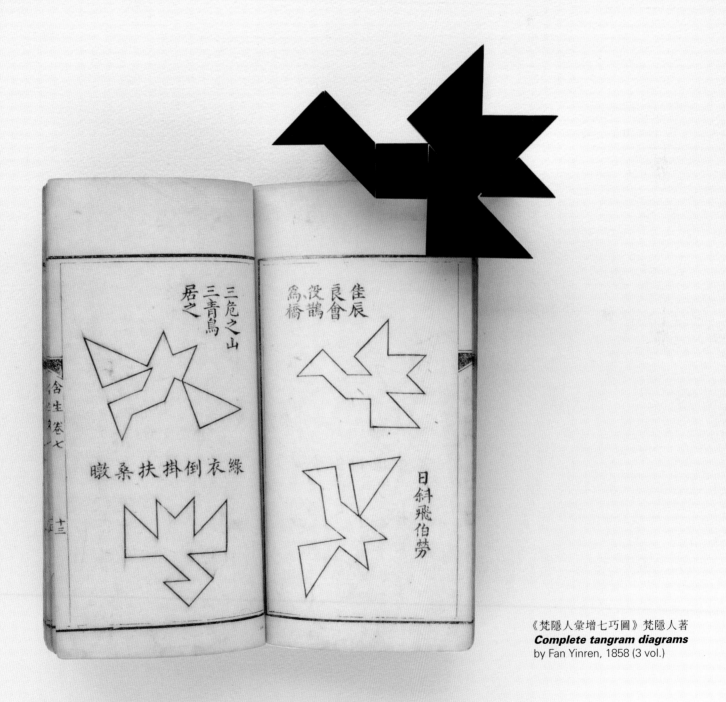

《梵隱人彙增七巧圖》梵隱人著
Complete tangram diagrams
by Fan Yinren, 1858 (3 vol.)

紫沙七巧調色盤
Paint dish with tangram design
Yixing stoneware with crackled white glaze
Yixing, Jiangsu Province;
Republic period (1911–1949)

Here the maker has used the tangram shapes
as a design motif, and there are no longer any
movable pieces.

瓷製七巧調色盤
Tangram-shaped paint dishes and box
Porcelain with painted enamels
Jingdezhen, Jiangxi Province;
Qing dynasty, 19th century

木製七巧板
Tangram pieces in finely carved box
Sandalwood
Canton; Qing dynasty, 19th century

瓷製七巧果盤
Tangram condiment dish set
Porcelain with colored enamels
Jingdezhen, Jiangxi Province;
Qing dynasty, Tongzhi reign (1862–1874)

These dishes, arranged in a square, were used to serve candies, nuts and dried fruits to guests during the Chinese New Year.

畫琺瑯七巧果盤
Tangram condiment dish set
Canton enamel
Canton; Qing dynasty, 19th century

This set of dishes is decorated with the eight Buddhist symbols (conch shell, umbrella, canopy, lotus, vase, pair of fish, endless knot, wheel of the law) plus a bat carrying a *shou* 壽 (longevity) character. The Chinese word for bat is *fu* 蝠, which puns with the word for fortune, *fu* 福. So a bat carrying a *shou* signifies longevity and good fortune. Can you identify all the Buddhist symbols?

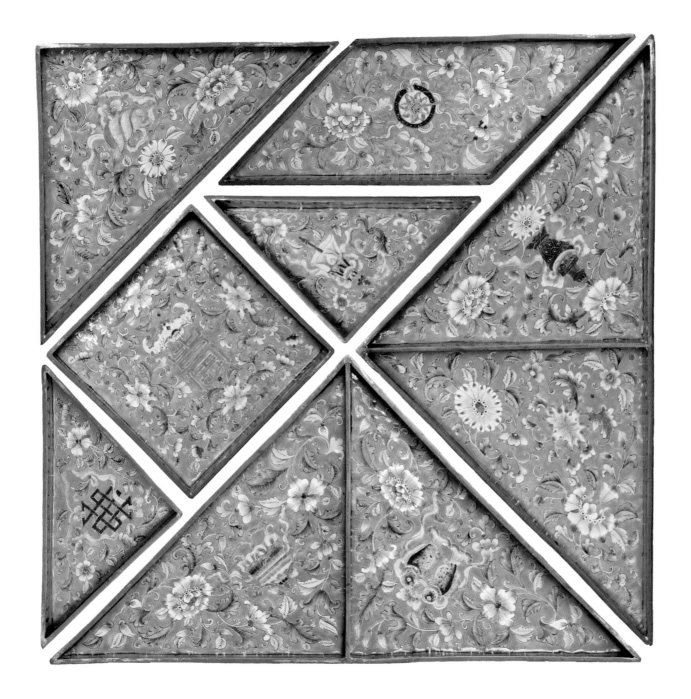

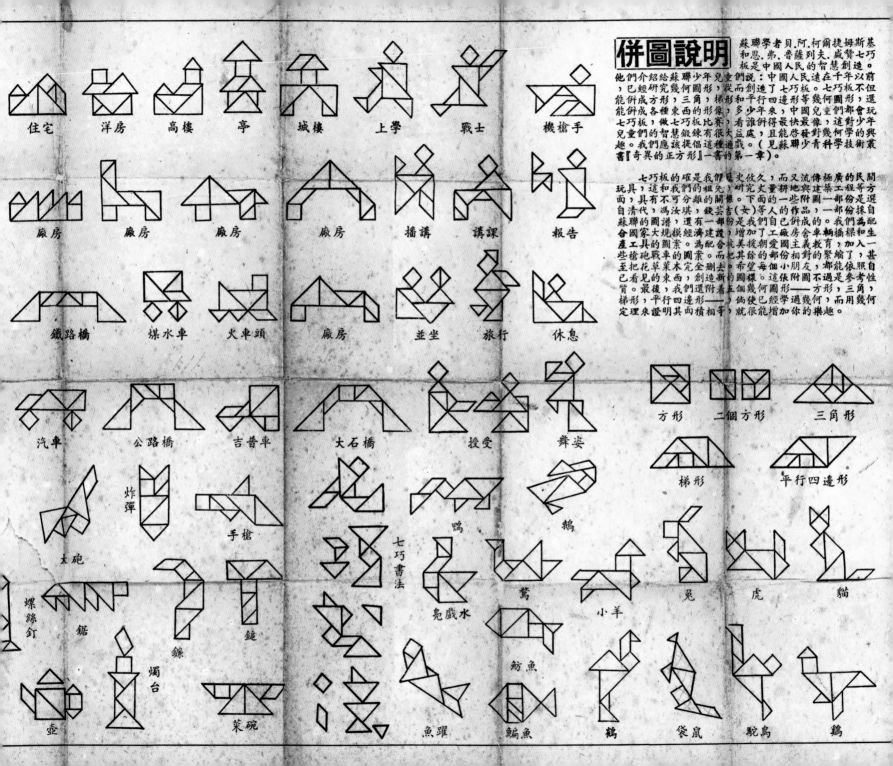

併圖說明

蘇聯學者.貝.阿.柯爾捷姆斯基和恩.弗.魯薩列夫.威贊七巧板是中國人民的智慧創造。

他們介紹給蘇聯少年兒童們說：中國人民遠在千年以前，已經研究幾何圖形，從而創造了七巧板。七巧板不但能併成方形，三角，梯形和平行四邊形等幾何圖形，還能併成各種東西的形像，多少年來，中國兒童們都會玩七巧板，做七巧板比賽，看誰併得最快最像，這對少年兒童們的智慧鍛鍊有很大益處，且能啟發對幾何學的興趣。我們應該提倡這種遊戲。（見蘇聯少青科學技術叢書『奇異的正方形』一書的第一章）。

七巧板的確是我們歷史攸久，而又流傳極廣的民間玩具，這和我們的祖先，研究丈量耕地與建築工程等方面，具有不可分離的關係。下面的一些附圖一部份是選自清代，馮汝琪，錢芸吉（女）等人的作品，一部份採自蘇聯的圖譜，還有一部份是我們自己併成的。我們為配合國家大規模經濟建設，增加了工廠房舍車輛橋標和生產工具的圖素。為配合抗美援朝愛國主義教育，加入一些槍砲戰車的圖素。而把其餘的部份相對的緊縮了，甚至把花草草木完全删去。希望每個小朋友，都能依照自己看見的東西，創造新的圖樣。這張附圖不過是參考性質。最後，我們附着五個幾何圖形——方形，三角，梯形，平行四邊形——倘使已經學過幾何，而用幾何定理來證明其面積相等，就很能增加你的樂趣。

住宅　洋房　高樓　亭　城樓　上學　戰士　機槍手

廠房　廠房　廠房　廠房　播講　講課　報告

鐵路橋　煤水車　火車頭　廠房　並坐　旅行　休息

汽車　公路橋　吉普車　大石橋　授受　舞姿

方形　二個方形　三角形

梯形　平行四邊形

大砲　炸彈　手槍　鵬　鵝

螺絲釘　鋸　鐮　鋤　七巧書法　鵞　鷺　小羊　兔　虎　貓

壺　燭台　菜碗　魚躍　鳧戲水　魴魚　鯿魚　鶴　袋鼠　駝鳥　雞

七巧圖說明
Sheet of tangram diagrams
Shanghai; 1950s

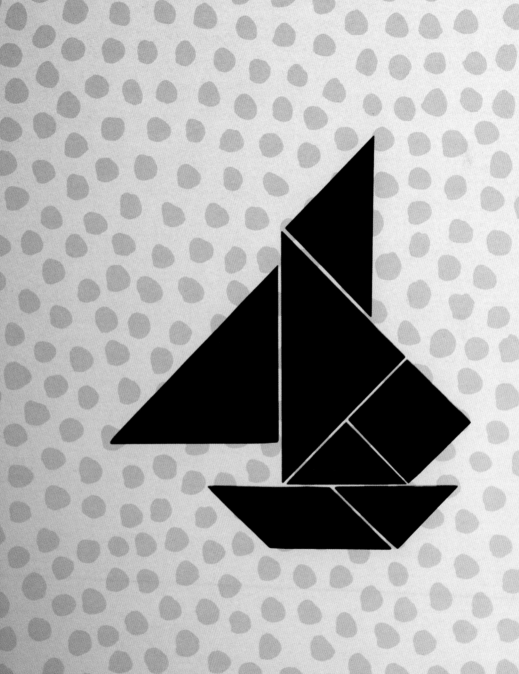

益智板

2. Fifteen-Piece Puzzle

銅及木製益智板
Fifteen-piece puzzles
Brass, wood
China; late 19th–early 20th century

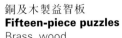

《益智圖》童叶庚著
Fifteen-piece puzzle diagrams
by Tong Xiegeng,
Hangzhou, 1878 (2 vol.)

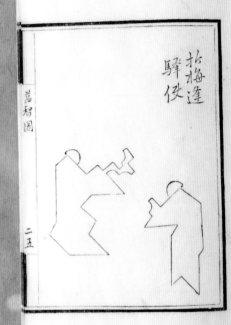

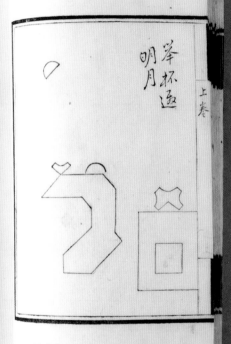

*As I broke off a prunus twig,
the messenger arrived…*

Raising my cup, I toast the moon…

In 1862 — almost 50 years after the earliest known tangram book was published — Tong Xiegeng (1828–1899), a scholar-official from Hangzhou, invented a 15-piece puzzle, which he called *yizhi ban* (enhancing intelligence pieces).

Six of the 15 pieces had curved edges, and this allowed Tong to construct very expressive illustrations of passages from literary classics. Tong published his two-volume *Yizhi tu* (Enhancing intelligence diagrams) in 1878, and he added two more volumes in 1885.

Next Tong took on his most ambitious project — using his 15 pieces to form the 1000 characters in the Liang dynasty (502–557) literacy primer *Qianziwen* (Thousand character essay). In 1892, he completed his eight-volume *Yizhi tu qianziwen* with diagrams for all 1000 characters.

七巧書出版五十年後，清代杭州學者童叶庚 (1828–1899) 發明了一個新的十五巧遊戲，並將這個遊戲稱作益智圖。

益智圖中的六個帶弧形的小片，使其更具有表達力。童叶庚用益智板為古典詩文配畫。他分別在 1878 和 1885 年出版了《益智圖》和《益智圖續集》。接下來，他用益智板拼出梁代 (502–557)《千字文》中所有的一千個字，並在 1892 年出版了《益智圖千字文》。

圖案取自童叶庚著《益智圖千字文》
Characters for *yi* (enhancing) and *zhi* (intelligence)
from *Thousand character diagrams*
by Tong Xiegeng, Shanghai, 1923

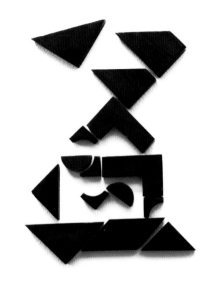

伏羲時龍馬
負圖出孟河，
背有陰陽
五十五點。
伏羲則之，
始畫八卦。

Dragon horse

獨釣寒江雪

Fishing alone in the river on a cold snowy day

圖案取自童叶庚著《益智圖》
Arrangements from *Fifteen-piece puzzle diagrams*
by Tong Xiegeng, Hangzhou, 1878

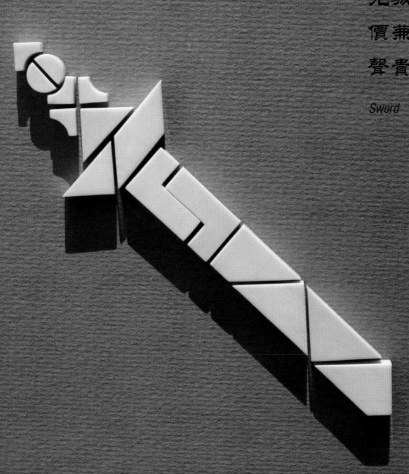

形震薛蜀，
光駭風胡。
價兼三鄉，
聲貴兩都。

Sword

九連環

3. Nine Linked Rings

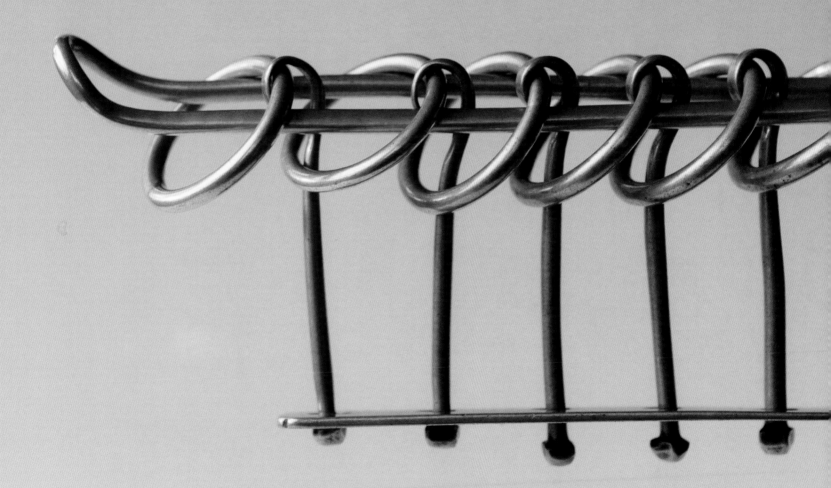

銅製九連環
Nine linked rings
Brass
China; 19th–20th century

銅製九連環
Nine linked rings
Brass
Hancheng, Shaanxi Province; 19th–20th century

The nine linked rings *(jiulianhuan)* is China's greatest puzzle. It consists of a looped handle that is interlocked with nine rings. The puzzle's objective is to remove all nine rings from the handle, and its solution takes 341 moves.

Although Chinese fascination with linked rings dates back more than 7000 years, Ming dynasty writer Yang Shen (1488–1559) made the earliest known reference to the nine linked rings puzzle. Later, Cao Xueqin (1715–1763) mentioned the puzzle in his Qing dynasty classic, *Dream of the Red Chamber*. And in 1821, Zhu Xiang Zhuren published a clever chart showing the puzzle's complete solution. Lots of patience is required to remove the nine rings from the handle. But there's a method to the solution — *and once you learn it, you'll never forget it!*

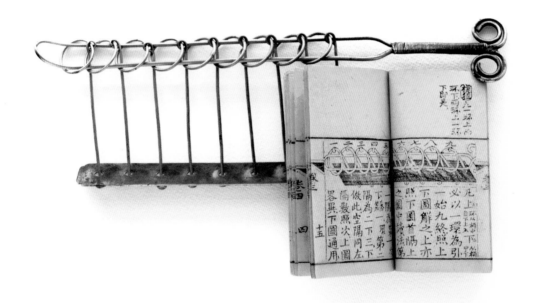

銀製九連環
Nine linked rings
Silver alloy
China; 19th–20th century

《小慧集》貯香主人著
Little wisdoms
by Zhu Xiang Zhuren, [1821?] (6 vol.)

This book of activities for young ladies contains
an ingenious solution to the nine linked rings.

九連環可能是中國最傑出的益智遊戲了。它由九個相連的環體和一個柄組成。解連環就是要將柄從環體中解出。解開所有九個環則要 341 步。

雖然在七千年前中國就有了連環，但是，九連環的起源很難考正。明代的楊慎 (1488–1559) 提到九連環是"閨婦孩童以為玩具"。曹雪芹 (1715–1763) 在《紅樓夢》中也講到賈寶玉和林黛玉在解九連環玩。道光 (1821–1850) 年間由貯香主人出版的《小慧集》中也介紹了九連環和其解法。玩這個遊戲要有耐心，一旦理解其結構，學會解法，就不會忘記！

妙緒環生《吳友如畫寶》
Ingenious undertaking of rings, ca. 1890
Wu Youru (Chinese, d. 1893)
From *Complete prints of Wu Youru*, Shanghai, 1909

銅製九連環
Nine linked rings
Brass, woven silk, ivory
China; 19th–20th century

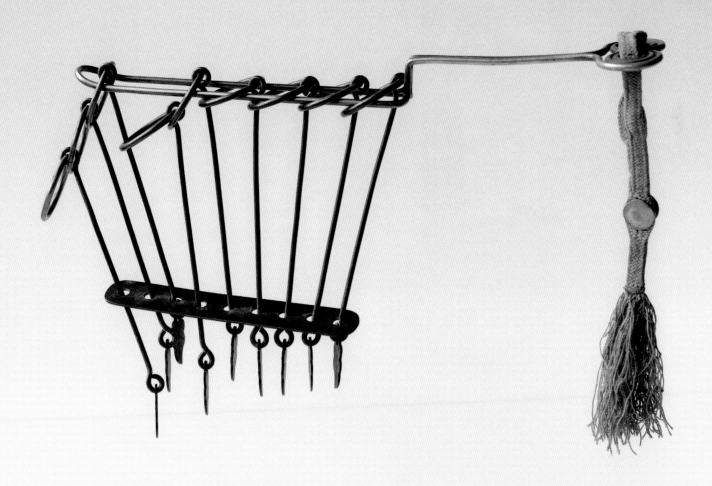

Ruan Liuqi in 1955 with his wire puzzle creations
in front of Suzhou's Renmin Market

二十世紀三十年代，蘇州的糖果商販阮劉琪看到一些孩子們在玩九連環和其它解環遊戲。他也開始製作九連環遊戲，在他的攤上銷售。阮劉琪同時也開始根據普通的器物的造形創作一些新的解環遊戲。這些巧環造形各異，有二十多種。接下來的三十多年，阮劉琪製作巧環並在蘇州的學校門口和人民市場上銷售。

一九五六年，蘇州中學的老師俞崇恩在學校門口看到了阮劉琪和他的巧環。俞崇恩對巧環產生了興趣，並在 1958 年寫了一本題為《巧環》的書，介紹阮劉琪的巧環。現在阮劉琪後代繼承了他的巧環事業，他們手工製作的阮氏巧環名揚中國。

In the 1930s, Ruan Liuqi, a candy vendor in Suzhou, noticed some children playing with a nine linked rings puzzle, and he started making and selling them. He then created similar wire puzzles in the shapes of common objects and soon had dozens of interesting designs. Ruan's puzzles became known as "ingenious rings."

For almost 30 years, Ruan Liuqi made wire puzzles and sold them near schools and at the Suzhou market. Today his descendants carry on his craft, and their handmade ingenious rings puzzles are famous all over China.

巧環 阮根全製作
Ingenious rings
Copper wire
Made by Ruan Genquan, son of Ruan Liuqi
Wuxi, Jiangsu Province; 1998

"If someone wanted a puzzle in the shape of a teapot, we made a teapot; if they wanted an airplane, we made an airplane…"

華
容
道

4. Sliding Block Puzzle

木製華容道
Sliding block puzzle
Softwood
Shanghai; Republic period, 1930s

The handwritten solution is one user's attempt to solve this puzzle.

木製華容道
Sliding block puzzle
Softwood
Shanghai; Republic period, 1930s

Huarong Pass *(Huarong Dao)* is a military strategy puzzle that became very popular in China during the late 1930s and early 1940s. The puzzle is named after a famous battle that occurred just prior to the Three Kingdoms period (220–280).

The rectangular board is a battlefield; the large square tile is the warlord Cao Cao; the other nine tiles are opposing commanders and soldiers; and the opening at the bottom of the board is Huarong Pass.

Initially the tiles are arranged with Cao Cao blocked by Guan Yu (represented by the horizontal rectangular tile) and his forces. Can you slide the tiles horizontally and vertically so that Cao Cao can eventually escape through the pass?

華容道是一個以三國故事為背景的軍事戰略滑塊遊戲，它在三、四十年代在中國非常流行。

華容道的"戰場"是一個長方形的托盤，托盤上一個大方滑塊代表三國人物曹操，其它九個滑塊代表要擒拿曹操的將士，托盤底部的開口是華容道出口。遊戲開始時，曹操被困，九個將士將他包圍。怎樣移動這些滑塊，才能幫助曹操逃脫呢？

三江口周瑜縱火，
燒赤壁曹操受困。
諸葛亮四面伏兵，
關雲長華容解圍。

Zhou Yu started a fire at the mouth of the three rivers.
The flames at Red Cliffs trapped Cao Cao,
And he was encircled by Zhuge Liang's soldiers,
But Guan Yunchang (Guan Yu) let him escape at Huarong Pass.

木製華容道
Sliding block puzzle
Softwood
Shanghai; Republic period, 1930s

38

紅木華容道
Sliding block puzzle
Hongmu
Changzhou, Jiangsu Province; Republic period, 1930s

Because of an obligation once incurred,
he opened the lock and set the dragon free.

5. Burr Puzzles

魯班鎖也叫"六子連芳"。它的用意是用六塊中間凹凸的木條拼成一個立體的結構。當這個結構快拼好時，要用最後一根木條將這個結構"鎖住"，使其穩定。人們可以發現它的結構和中國建築及傢俱中的榫卯結構有異曲同功之妙。

魯班是中國古代最聰明的木匠。但是魯班鎖是誰發明的已無可考證。不難推測它是中國古代木匠用剩餘木料所製的玩具。魯班鎖的結構還出現在一些實用物品上，如：掛件、練手球、線板和筷子簍等。

Burr puzzles are made of interlocking rods that are assembled into geometrically pleasing structures. When a structure is almost complete, the last rod is slid in or rotated to "lock" the other rods in place. The notched joints of a burr puzzle are similar to the joinery used in traditional Chinese furniture and architecture.

We don't know when the first Chinese burr puzzles were created, but it's easy to imagine traditional woodworkers using scraps of leftover wood to make these puzzles for amusement. What we do know is that burr puzzles have assumed distinctly Chinese forms as toggles, hand-exercise balls, yarn winders and chopsticks holders. In China, burr puzzles are called *Lu Ban suo* (Lu Ban locks) in honor of Lu Ban, the patron saint of carpentry.

木製魯班鎖
Wooden six-piece burr puzzle
China; 19th–20th century

《中外戲法圖說》 唐芸洲著
Chinese and Western magic with diagrams
by Tang Yunzhou, Suzhou, 1895 (6 vol.)

In China, magic, puzzles and acrobatics are related pursuits. So it's not surprising to find puzzles in a magic book.

竹木製魯班鎖結構筷子簍
Chopsticks holder
Bamboo, softwood
Southern China; 19th–20th century

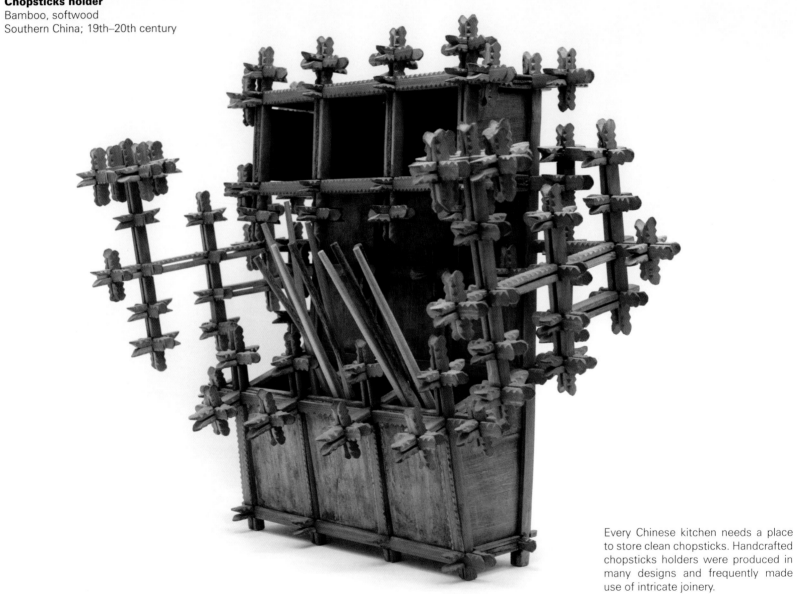

Every Chinese kitchen needs a place to store clean chopsticks. Handcrafted chopsticks holders were produced in many designs and frequently made use of intricate joinery.

木製魯班鎖結構繞線板
Wooden yarn winders
Shanxi Province; 19th–20th century

How many colors of yarn could be kept on one of these yarn winders? Although their joints are the same as those used in interlocking puzzles, yarn winders weren't meant to be taken apart.

連環戒指

6. Puzzle Rings and Bracelets

新打戒指九連環，一個連環交九年；
九九還歸八十一，還愛相交十九年。

— 客家民歌

I had a nine-linked ring made, and each ring stands for nine years.
That totals 81 years, and I'll continue loving you for another 19 years...

— Hakka folk song

銀製連環戒指
Nine-band puzzle ring
Silver, enamel
Northern China;
Qing dynasty, 18th–19th century

Puzzle rings are finger rings with four or more linked bands that can be spread apart when the ring is removed from the finger. But once apart, the bands are very difficult to reassemble into a ring.

連環戒指通常由四個或更多的連環組成。這些連環可以散開或還原成戒指。但是，一旦散開後，將戒指還原頗為困難。

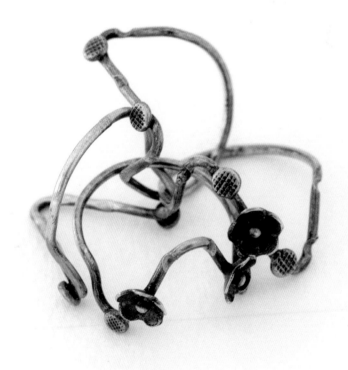

銀製連環戒指
Four-band puzzle ring
Silver, enamel
Northern China;
Qing dynasty, 18th–19th century

It's possible that puzzle rings were originally brought to China from West Asia over the Silk Road. While the imported puzzle rings would have had plain bands, the Chinese added decorations and changed them into artistic creations.

連環戒指很有可能是從西亞由絲綢之路傳入中國。西亞的連環戒指常是素環相連，而中國的連環戒指卻富有各種民間寓意的裝飾。

銀製連環戒指
Four-band puzzle rings
Silver, enamel, ivory
Northern China;
Qing dynasty, 18th–19th century

Qing dynasty silversmiths embellished most puzzle rings with auspicious symbols that expressed people's wishes for happiness, successful careers, longevity or many descendants.

Blessings, rank and longevity: The three Daoist star gods — Fu (the god of blessings), Lu (the god of rank), and Shou (the god of longevity) — symbolize the most basic Chinese wishes.

Male descendants: *Gua* 瓜 is a melon, which has many seeds, and *die* 蝶 (butterfly) puns with *die* 瓞 (small melon). The rebus reads as *guadie mianmian* 瓜瓞綿綿 (may you have ceaseless generations of sons and grandsons).

Good fortune and longevity: The word for bat in Chinese is *fu* 蝠, which puns with the word for fortune, *fu* 福. Here two bats are flanking a stylized longevity character.

Happiness: When magpies (*xique* 喜鵲) and plum blossoms (*meihua* 梅花) are shown together, the resulting rebus reads in Chinese as *xi shang mei shao* 喜上梅梢 (magpies fly to the top of the plum tree). This puns with the expression *xi shang mei shao* 喜上眉梢 (may happiness reach up to the top of your eyebrows, or, may you be filled with happiness).

Reference: Terese Tse Bartholomew, *Hidden Meanings in Chinese Art* (San Francisco: Asian Art Museum, 2006).

Most Chinese puzzle rings have four bands or nine bands. Puzzle bracelets were also made with five bands or seven bands.

大多的中國的連環戒指由四個或九個連環組成。連環手鐲則是由五個或七個連環組成。

銀製七連環手鐲一對
Pair of seven-band puzzle bracelets
Silver
Northern China; Qing dynasty, 18th–19th century

7. Puzzle Locks

Chinese metal padlocks were already in production during the Western Wei dynasty (535–557), and their basic structure remained the same until they were replaced by Western-style locks in the 20th century.

Traditional padlocks are secured by internal springs that must be compressed by the key in order to open. Most padlocks are easy to open, but others were specially designed to outwit lock pickers. Some of these "puzzle locks" have cleverly hidden keyholes, while others open in several stages requiring many steps.

Traditional combination locks were invented much later than spring locks. To open a combination lock one must rotate several disks until a row of pictures or characters lines up to form the correct combination.

中國在西魏 (535–557) 或更早的時期就有了金屬的簧片鎖。它們自始至終保持著這種基本結構，直到二十世紀初才被西方的鎖具所取代。

傳統的中國鎖芯是一組金屬簧片，開鎖時則需用鑰匙將這些簧片壓下去。大部分的傳統中國鎖都很容易打開。但是，有一些卻讓人們頗費周折。這些益智鎖具各有千秋，需要有智慧的人們才可以打開。

傳統的中國密碼鎖比簧片鎖出現要晚得多。它需要先將鎖輪上的圖形或文字對好，才能打開。

雙鑰匙鎖
Two-key lock
Brass
China; 19th–20th century

隱秘鎖孔鎖
Hidden keyhole lock
Brass
China; 19th–20th century

You have the key, but the lock doesn't seem to have a keyhole. After some time you discover how to rotate a secret panel to reveal a hidden slot. Then just insert the key and push the lock open.

迷宮鎖
Maze lock
Brass
China; 19th–20th century

You see the lock's strange keyhole, but the key won't go in. After much frustration the key finally enters, and the lock easily opens.

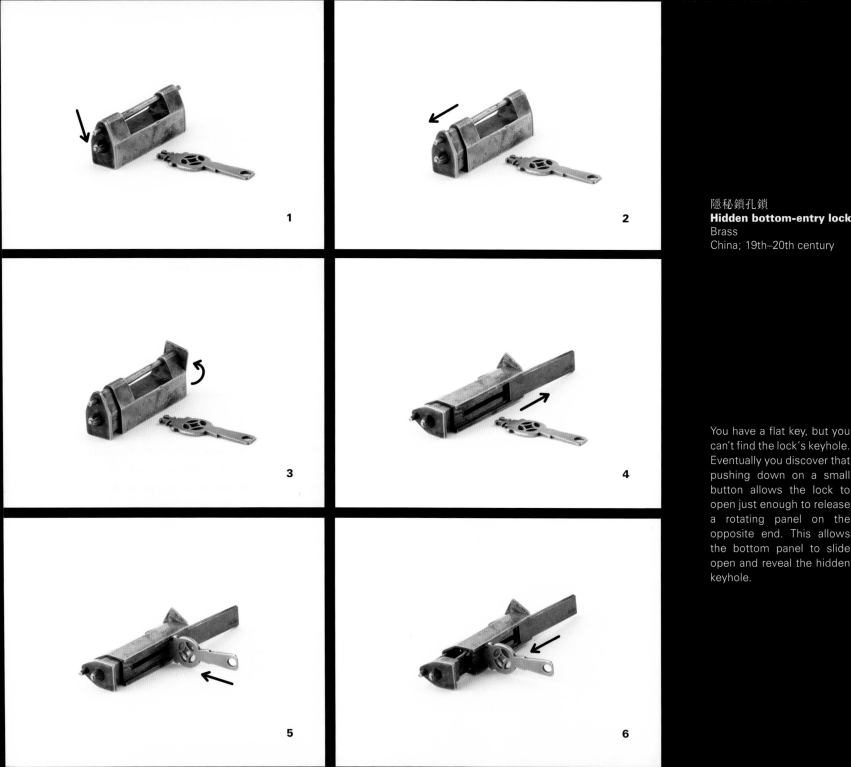

1

2

隱秘鎖孔鎖
Hidden bottom-entry lock
Brass
China; 19th–20th century

3

4

You have a flat key, but you can't find the lock's keyhole. Eventually you discover that pushing down on a small button allows the lock to open just enough to release a rotating panel on the opposite end. This allows the bottom panel to slide open and reveal the hidden keyhole.

5

6

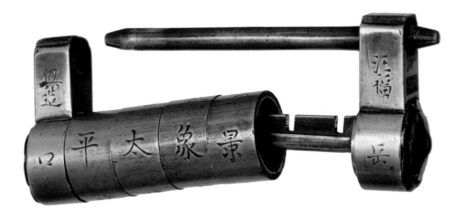

密碼鎖
Combination lock
Brass (top)
Yuekou, Hubei Province; 19th–20th century

密碼鎖
Combination locks
Brass (bottom left), silver alloy (bottom right)
China; 19th–20th century

中國貿易遊戲

8. Puzzles for Export

WAH LOONG,
FROM CANTON,
DEALER IN SILKS,
Crape Shawls, Ivory
and Lacquered Ware Matting,
No. 60 Queen's Road.

CUMWO

WAH LO
AN
CUM

We all know that present-day China is the world's leading toy manufacturer. But did you know that over 200 years ago Chinese craftsmen were already creating ivory toys, games and puzzles especially for export to the West?

During the late 18th and early 19th centuries, foreign traders who sailed to China to purchase tea, silk, porcelain and other products were restricted to a small strip of waterfront outside Canton's city wall. Dozens of small Chinese shops catered to these foreign buyers' personal needs, including several that offered intricately carved ivory puzzles. In addition to individual puzzles, the Canton dealers also sold large sets of ivory puzzles, games and toys, which they packaged in custom-fitted lacquer boxes.

大家都知道，現在的中國是世界上生產玩具的大國。可是你知道嗎？在兩百年以前，中國就有用象牙製作的玩具出口到西方了。

十八世紀末至十九世紀初，西方的商船來中國購買茶葉、絲綢、瓷器等。那時商人們只能在廣州城外特定的交易區購物。那裡有幾十家商鋪為外商們服務，其中就有專營象牙制品和玩具的商鋪。除了零售象牙玩具，廣州的商人們還為外商們定做成套的象牙玩具，用漆盒盛置。

香港象牙製品店 照片
Chinese Curio Shop, Hong Kong, 1870
by John Thomson (Scottish, 1837–1921)

John Thomson was one of the first photographers to provide real images of China to the outside world. Here we see the interior of a typical 19th century ivory shop that catered to Westerners. How many puzzles can you find on the shelves?

外銷象牙製益智遊戲
Puzzles and games made for export
Ivory, silk thread and brass in lacquer box
Canton; Qing dynasty, 19th century

四喜

9. The Four-Happiness Boys

Do you see four boys in these pictures? If not, then look again!

This traditional Chinese folk design is known as "four happiness" *(sixi)*. It symbolizes good fortune and happiness and is often used to celebrate a new birth. The four-happiness boys are one of several Chinese visual puzzles in which humans or animals share body parts.

Legend has it that during the early Ming dynasty (1368–1644) a child prodigy created this design to represent the happiness of the farmer who sees rain after a long drought, the happiness of a traveler who meets a fellow countryman in a distant land, the happiness of the first night of marriage, and the happiness of heading the court examination results list.

四喜圖繪瓷盒
Powder box with "four-happiness boys" motif
Porcelain with underglaze blue and colored enamels
China; Qing dynasty, Kangxi period (1662–1722)

數數看，這個圖裡有四個孩子嗎？如果沒有，那就再仔細數數。

這個傳統的圖畫叫四喜，也叫四喜娃，是中國民間的吉祥圖畫。這個圖形代表福運和喜慶，特別是象徵多子多孫，常用在祝賀新生兒的禮箱上。四喜圖是中國趣味益智圖形的一種。

傳說這個造型是明代 (1368–1644) 神童解縉創作的。俗稱"四喜"代表了：

久旱逢甘雨，
他鄉遇故知，
洞房花燭夜，
金榜題名時。

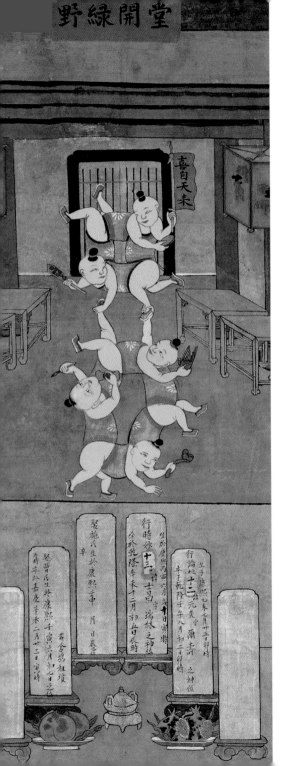

銅製四喜鎮紙
Paperweight in the form of "four-happiness boys"
Brass
China; Ming dynasty (1368–1644)

祖宗像上的四喜和六子圖（局部）
Ancestor portrait with many boys (detail)
Paint and ink on silk
China; Qing dynasty, 18th century

How many boys do you see?

四喜多子圖繪瓷茶葉罐
Tea caddy and cover
Porcelain with colored enamels
China; Republic period, 1934

Here's a popular variation of
the four-happiness boys image.
How many boys can you count?

四喜多子圖繪瓷茶壺
Teapot and cover
Porcelain with colored enamels,
silver alloy handle
China; Republic period, ca. 1934

益智容器

10. Puzzle Vessels

This wine pot doesn't have an opening on top, but it can be filled through a hole in its bottom.

Surprisingly — because of its ingenious construction — it's possible to turn the pot upright when full without spilling any wine. Can you solve the puzzle of how it works?

The earliest known bottom-filling wine pot *(dao liu hu)* was made in the Tang dynasty (618–906). During the Ming (1368–1644) and Qing (1644–1911) dynasties, most of these pots were formed in the shape of a peach — a symbol of long life — and made very appropriate birthday gifts. They also became popular export items, known in the West as "Cadogan teapots."

怎樣才能將酒註入一個沒有蓋的酒壺？

把壺倒過來從壺底倒灌進去！

奇怪的是當酒壺放正時，壺內的酒卻不會流出來。這是為甚麼？
壺內的結構是怎樣的呢？

倒流壺早在唐代 (618–906) 就有了。到了明 (1368–1644) 清 (1644–1911) 時期，大部分的倒流壺是桃形的。桃子有祝福長壽的預意，因此，桃形的倒流壺常是壽辰（生日）時的壽禮和酒具。倒流壺隨外貿瓷傳到西方，被稱為 "Cadogan teapots"。

瓷倒流壺
Bottom-filling wine pot
Porcelain with celadon, iron red and underglaze blue
Jingdezhen, Jiangxi Province; Qing dynasty, Qianlong period (1736–1795)

The phoenix spreads its wings for ten thousand li;
Colorful clouds toast the new wine of a hundred seasons.

金天聚造　錫製倒流壺
Bottom-filling wine pot
Pewter
Made by Jin Tian Jü
China; late Qing dynasty (1644–1911)

1, 2

3

4

5

6

7

8

9

10

粗瓷倒流醋壺
Bottom-filling vinegar pots
Pottery with green enamel and underglaze blue
Shanxi Province; mid-20th century

Shanxi people are known for their love of sorghum-based vinegar. These bottom-filling
vinegar pots can be dated by the political slogans of the times.

1. 味五和調　　mixing in harmony the five spices (written right to left), before 1950

2. 調和五味　　mixing in harmony the five spices (written left to right), after 1950

3. 菊有秋香　　chrysanthemum flowers give autumn scent, 1950s

4. 菊竹梅蘭　　chrysanthemum, bamboo, prunus and orchid, 1950s

5. 澤光普照　　the luster of light shines everywhere on earth, 1950s

6. 百花齊放　　let a hundred flowers bloom, 1957

7. 自力更生　　self-reliance, 1960s

8. 奮發圖強　　struggle to be strong, 1960s

9. 慶祝豐收　　celebrating a bumper harvest, 1961

10. 斗私批修　　struggle against selfishness and criticize revisionism, 1969

Here's a cup that teaches the classical Chinese paradigm that modesty brings gain and arrogance results in loss. Hence its name: fairness cup *(gong dao bei)*.

Fill the cup half way...no problem. But take more than your share of wine...and every drop drains out through a hole in the bottom. How does it work?

Mounted inside the cup is a hollow human figure. Inside the figure is a tube attached to a hole through the bottom of the cup. Wine enters a hidden hole at the foot of the hollow figure. When the wine's level reaches the top of the tube it is all siphoned out of the cup.

The earliest known fairness cup was made during the Song dynasty (960–1279).

這個杯子教人"謙受益,滿招損",所以叫公道杯。

先將酒註入杯裡一半,沒有問題。但是,當酒倒得太滿時,杯中所有的酒都會流出。這是怎麼一回事呢?

在杯子裡有一個空心人物,裡面有一根細管和杯底的小洞相連。杯中註入酒時,酒就會從人腳下的一個小口進入人體,當酒液面高出細管的頂部時,虹吸就會將酒"吸"出杯外。

現存最早的公道杯是宋代 (960–1279) 的。

瓷公道杯
Fairness cup
Porcelain with celadon and underglaze blue
Jingdezhen, Jiangxi Province;
Qing dynasty, Qianlong period (1736–1795)

瓷公道杯
Fairness cup
Porcelain with colored enamels
Jingdezhen, Jiangxi Province;
Qing dynasty, Qianlong period (1736–1795)

紫沙公道杯
Fairness cup
Yixing stoneware
Yixing, Jiangsu Province;
Qing dynasty, late 19th century

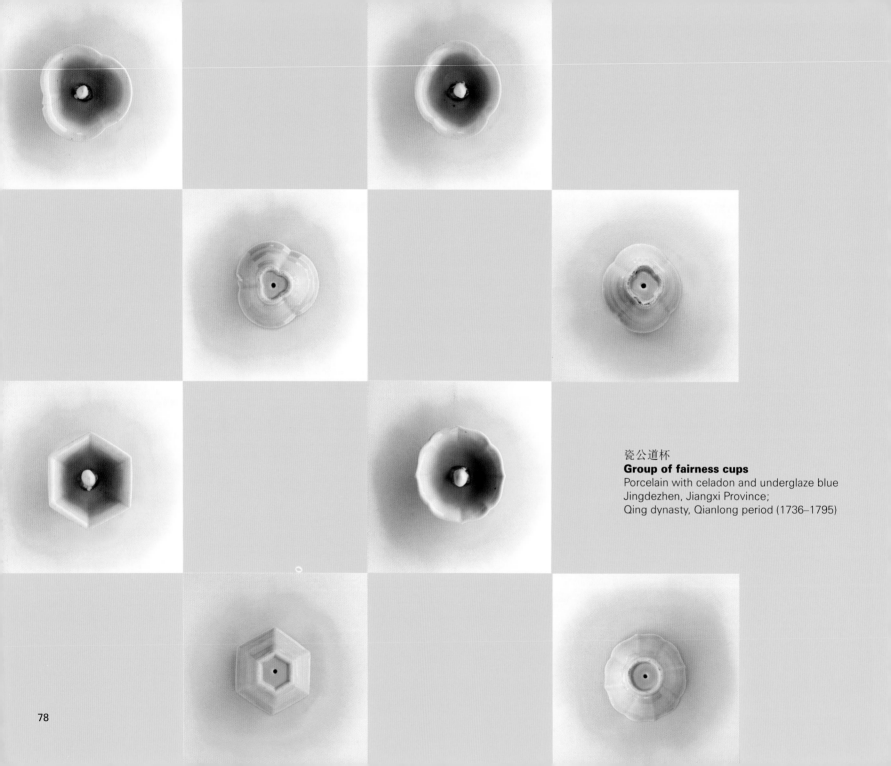

瓷公道杯
Group of fairness cups
Porcelain with celadon and underglaze blue
Jingdezhen, Jiangxi Province;
Qing dynasty, Qianlong period (1736–1795)

瓷公道杯
Fairness cup
Porcelain with celadon and blue glaze
Jingdezhen, Jiangxi Province;
Qing dynasty, Qianlong period (1736–1795)